A Catholic Bishop Responds...

# A Will to Live:
# Clear Answers on
# End of Life Issues

## Most Reverend José H. Gomez, STD

BASILICA ™
P R E S S

Published by Basilica Press
111 Ferguson Court Suite 102
Irving, TX 75062

Scripture verses contained herein are from
*The Catholic Family Bible*, The Catholic Press, Inc.,
Chicago, 1966

Editors:        Lynn Klika and Brian O'Neel
Cover design:   Giuliana Gerber / ACI Prensa

Printed in the United States of America
ISBN 1-930314-06-X

Basilica Press is part of the
Joseph and Marie Daou Foundation.

# CONTENTS

# INTRODUCTION

The reasons for this booklet…

Throughout my life as a priest and bishop, I have met death on many occasions.

I have assisted many Catholics, young and old, on their deathbeds by administering the final sacraments to them. I have witnessed violent and unexpected death, as well as death which has come after a long waiting period. I have had to console countless family members of the deceased, and I have also been the final witness at the death of the desolate. It doesn't matter how often one encounters death or the various ways in which it occurs. It is impossible to get used to it, to consider it as something "normal." Death is a mystery that always deeply affects us.

Perhaps this is why many spiritual teachers from ages past have suggested that Christians should meditate on their own death, not to paralyze us with fear, but rather to help us better appreciate our Christian life and to live it more fully.

By contrast, popular culture tries its best to avoid the topic of death. This is done not only through the desperate search for ways of prolonging life and avoiding death, which in itself isn't wrong, but through the desire to escape death as an unavoidable reality of life.

In a moving meditation, former Joseph Cardinal Ratzinger, today Pope Benedict XVI, wrote that modern culture tries to escape from the mystery of death in two ways.

The first, he wrote, is by ignoring it, "softening" its certainty to some degree. A good example is the decision of the editorial board of some American newspapers to actively eliminate the word "death" from their vocabulary. People "pass away," "are deceased" or some other thing, but they are never "dead."

The second way of escaping from the mystery of death is by rendering it so irrelevant that it loses its seriousness. A good example in this case is the action movie, in which the "bad guys" are eliminated like flies. Death thus becomes an exciting spectacle, a source of entertainment rather than of fear or compassion.

Nonetheless, all of us know that death, and particularly the idea of our own death, continually inspires in us a sense of fear and a fundamental questioning regarding the meaning of our own life.

This anxiety about death has always accompanied me as a priest and as a bishop, especially my mother's death. My mother suffered from Alzheimer's disease for almost a decade. I saw how the mental faculties of the person that so lovingly nurtured me diminished before my own eyes. Yet, the person that I embraced at her deathbed was still the same that embraced me countless times during my life.

These memories were awakened within me even more vividly some time ago, when the entire country and indeed the world witnessed with horror the death of Terri Schindler-Schiavo.

The death of this defenseless woman in a Florida hospice, brought about by those who claimed to want what was best for her and who proclaimed a "death with dignity" on her behalf, aroused a wave of doubt in many Catholics regarding the meaning of life and death, about our final hours, about what a dignified death really is and what it is not.

These concerns are legitimate. Catholic doctrine itself has been required to reflect upon and to define certain topics that never came to light in the past when they did not exist. Such is the case with modern technologies that prolong human life sometimes beyond what is reasonable or those that destroy it.

Therefore, I would like to offer a few reflections in the form of questions and answers, a format used so effectively in Catholic catechetical tradition. In doing so, I hope to help the faithful to better understand these topics so that even as we prepare for our own death, we will know how to act as true Catholics.

We bishops are teachers of the Truth. But this does not mean that we know everything there is to know about every topic. Therefore, I would like to express my gratitude to the following individuals for their valuable assistance in editing this booklet: Dr. Renzo Paccini, MD, bioethics specialist and former official of the Vatican Pontifical Council for Health Pastoral Care; Dr. Gustavo Sánchez, PhD, STL, professor of the College of Civil and Pontifical Theology (Facultad de Teología Pontificia y Civil) in Lima (Peru); and Dr. John M. Haas, PhD, STL, president of the National Catholic Bioethics Center. I commend the readers of this book to the care of St. Joseph, whom the Church venerates as patron of the sick and of a happy death. In doing so, it is my hope that by better understanding the mystery of death, we will be better able to live a Christian life.

Most Reverend José H. Gomez, STD
Archbishop of San Antonio, Texas

# I) What is life?

Life is defined as the existence of a being that possesses the ability to attain its full potential in accordance with its nature. Life involves dynamism, movement and development, all of which differentiate living beings from non-living ones, which are stiff and immobile. We human beings possess life because we have received it as a gift from God. In fact, He created us and gave us the gift of our existence so that we would attain an incomparable fullness: The vocation of being children of God (cf., Eph 1:3-4; Jn 1:10-12). Our life has a unique and supernatural goal: to achieve a loving communion with God. Human life is sacred (cf., the *Catechism of the Catholic Church*, 2258) because it is the fruit of God's creative action, and it remains forever in a very special relationship with the Creator. God not only created human beings, but He also sustains them, watches over them, protects them and loves them constantly.

# 2) What is death?

To the Christian, death is not the end of life, but rather a dramatic transition to a new state of being. Death involves a decisive step, and, therefore, fear of death is natural. At the same time, for the person of faith, it marks the transition into a definitive encounter with God, that marvelous moment for which we have all been created. Defining when death has occurred, however, is a task left to medical science.[1]

A competent scientist must conduct the necessary studies and investigation to determine "in the most precise way possible the exact moment and the irrefutable sign of death."[2]

The proof and the interpretation of these signs of physical death are left to the competence of medical science and not to morality or faith.[3]

Medically speaking, death is defined as the "permanent cessation of all vital functions." For this reason, the

---

[1] Pius XII, "Address on 'Reanimation'" (24 November 1957). On this occasion, the Holy Father said that "it is up to the doctor to give a clear and precise definition of *death* and the *moment of death* of a patient who expires in a state of unconsciousness."

[2] John Paul II, "Address to the Pontifical Academy of the Sciences on the Artificial Prolongation of Life and Determining the Precise Moment of Death," 6 (14 December 1989)

[3] Cf. Pontifical Council for Pastoral Assistance to Health Care Workers, *Charter for Health Care Workers*, p. 128 (Vatican City, 1995)

classic signs used to determine the moment of death have been the definitive shutdown of heart and lung function. In the majority of cases, this continues to be the main criterion used by doctors to diagnose and certify that death has occurred.[4]

Nonetheless, in recent times the use of resuscitation techniques and vital organ transplants have necessitated a more precise diagnosis of when death occurs.

Thus, beginning with the fact that one's death "is a single event, consisting of the total disintegration of that unitary and integrated whole that is the personal self,"[5] we can currently specify that a person "is dead when he has irreversibly lost all ability to integrate and coordinate the physical and mental functions of the body."[6]

Since the organ known as the diencephalon, located at the brain's posterior, integrates and coordinates the body's physical and mental functions, "brain death is the true criterion of death, although the definitive

---

[4]Charles B. Clayman, *The American Medical Association Encyclopedia of Medicine* (Random House, 1989)

[5]John Paul II, "Address to the 18th International Congress of the Transplantation Society," 4 (29 August 2000). See

http://www.vatican.va/holy_father/john_paul_ii/speeches/2000/jul-sep/documents/hf_jp-ii_spe_20000829_transplants_en.html

[6]Pontifical Academy of Sciences, *The Artificial Prolongation of Life and the Determination of the Exact Moment of Death* , 1 (October 1985)

arrest of cardio-respiratory activity very quickly leads to brain death."[7]

This knowledge has led from "classic" criteria for determining death to "neurological" criteria, in other words, what is known as brain death.

[7]Ibid.

# 3) What does brain death mean?

It is necessary to specify what the term brain death means.

Brain death is a term used to indicate that one has been determined to be dead using neurological criteria. It is "the complete and irreversible cessation of all brain activity (in the cerebrum, cerebellum and brain stem). This is then considered the sign that the individual organism has lost its integrative capacity."[8] Verifying that brain death has occurred according to this definition would permit the doctor to certify death in situations in which the lungs and heart continue functioning with the help of machines.[9]

In other words, the death of an organism as an entity (integral and coordinated) does not necessarily correlate with the death of all parts of the organism. To determine death by a rigorous and objective ascertaining of the moment when all activity of the cerebrum, cerebellum and brain stem has completely and irreversibly stopped does not conflict with proper

---

[8] John Paul II, "Address to the 18th International Congress of the Transplantation Society," 5. It is important to emphasize that the definition for *brain* is understood not only as the *cerebrum*, but rather all structures of the nervous system as a whole that are contained within the cranium and are universally known as the "encephalon:" the cerebrum, the cerebellum and the brain stem. Otherwise, the definition would be invalid.
[9] E. Wijdicks, "Brain Death," *New England Journal of Medicine*, 344, (2001): 1215-1221

Christian teaching regarding what a human person is.[10]

Therefore, "a health worker [who is] professionally responsible for ascertaining death can use these criteria in each individual case as the basis for arriving at that degree of assurance in ethical judgment which moral teaching describes as moral certainty."[11]

[10] Cf. John Paul II, "Address to the 18th International Congress of the Transplantation Society," 5
[11] Ibid.

# 4) What is a terminal illness?

Terminal illness is the stage of any illness, generally a long one, in which there is an irreversible deterioration in one's health condition that can no longer be reasonably forestalled by medical intervention and for which it is therefore determined that the patient has entered the final stage of his earthly existence. [12]

For the terminally ill, "life is particularly and progressively precarious and painful. To illness and physical suffering is added the psychological and spiritual drama of detachment which death signifies and implies."[13]

For this reason, the terminally ill are particularly in need of human and Christian companionship.

---

[12] Cf. Pontifical Council for Pastoral Assistance, *Charter*, p. 115. See also Lawrence M. Tierney, Stephen J. McPhee, Maxine A. Papadakis, *Current Medical Diagnosis & Treatment* (McGraw Hill, 2003), p. 60

[13] Pontifical Council for Pastoral Assistance, *Charter*, p. 115

## 5) What is a degenerative disorder?

The expression degenerative disorder or degenerative illness encompasses "a wide range of conditions in which there is a progressive impairment of both the structure and function of part of the body."[14]

The following are excluded from this list: infectious diseases and inflammatory diseases, as well as those due to immunological disturbances, chemical or physical changes or neoplastic diseases (i.e., cancer).

"Many of the signs of aging, such as wrinkling of the skin, are due to degenerative changes in body tissues; but in degenerative disorders, the changes come earlier in life, are more rapid, and typically affect some organs and not others,"[15] such as, for example, nerve tissue or muscles.

Some known examples of degenerative disorders are Parkinson's disease, Alzheimer's disease, multiple sclerosis and different muscular dystrophies.

The course of a degenerative disorder is progressive, though the rate varies depending on each illness.

---

[14] Clayman, *American Medical Association (AMA) Encyclopedia of Medicine.*
[15] Ibid.

# 6) What is the meaning of a vegetative state, and when is it permanent?

A vegetative state is a clinical condition of complete unawareness of the self and the environment, accompanied by one distinguishing clinical feature: Sleep-wake cycles (meaning that there are moments in which the patient opens his eyes). In a vegetative state the patient's basic body functions such as breathing, heartbeat and body temperature are maintained.[16] Moreover, occasional random movements of the head and limbs may occur. In this clinical condition there are no longer any signs of consciousness, and there is no response to stimuli.[17]

Drawing from scientific teaching, Pope John Paul II affirmed, "The person in a vegetative state, in fact, shows no evident sign of self-awareness or awareness of the environment, and seems unable to interact with others or to react to specific stimuli."[18]

---

[16] Cf. The Multi-Society Task Force on PVS [i.e., Persistent Vegetative State], "Medical Aspects of the Persistent Vegetative State / First of Two Parts," *The New England Journal of Medicine [aka, NEJM]*, 330, (1994): 1499-1508

[17] Clayman, *AMA Encyclopedia of Medicine*.

[18] John Paul II, "Address to the Participants in the International Congress on 'Life-Sustaining Treatments and Vegetative State: Scientific Advances and Ethical Dilemmas,'" 2 (20 March 2004). See http://www.vatican.va/holy_father/john_paul_ii/speeches/2004/march/docume nts/hf_jp-ii_spe_20040320_ congress-fiamc_en.html

Various factors can lead a person to a vegetative state, such as severe or chronic cerebral damage, progression of degenerative or metabolic neurological diseases or developmental malformations of the nervous system.[19]

A so-called vegetative state can be transitory; however, when it lasts for more than a year, it is then categorized as a permanent vegetative state.

This new definition does not imply a new medical diagnosis in the person (the diagnosis continues to be called a vegetative state). It merely offers us a specific piece of the prognosis based on probabilities, not on absolutes. It tells us that the patient's condition has become irreversible according to "the fact that the recovery of patients, statistically speaking, is ever more difficult as the condition of vegetative state is prolonged over time."[20]

Nevertheless, it must not be forgotten that medical records attest to quite a few people who have recovered with lesser or greater consequences from the so-called permanent vegetative state. We can therefore say that medical science is not yet in the position to predict with

---

[19] Cf. The Multi-Society Task Force on PVS, "Aspects of Persistent Vegetative State" *NEJM*, 1499-1508

[20] John Paul II, "Address to the Participants in the International Congress on 'Life-Sustaining Treatments and Vegetative State: Scientific Advances and Ethical Dilemmas,'" 2

certainty which patient will recover from this condition and which will not.

It's important to emphazise that the term "vegetative" is only used to describe a clinical state. Though use of this term is widespread and widely accepted, in no way should it or could it be applied to a sick person in the literal sense. That is, speaking of the patient as if he or she had really become a "vegetable" would demean his or her value and personal dignity.[21]

Acknowledging the risk of such serious confusion in the use and application of the term "vegetative," we must gratefully accept the apostolic exhortation of Pope John Paul II to "reaffirm strongly that the intrinsic value and personal dignity of every human being do not change, no matter what the concrete circumstances of his or her life."[22]

---

[21] Ibid.
[22] Ibid.

# 7) What is a comatose state?

A coma is a neurological condition related to a vegetative state, but it is not the same thing. Similar to a vegetative state, it also involves a deep, sustained pathologic unconsciousness (one that persists for at least an hour). Unlike a vegetative state, however, a coma does not involve sleep-wake cycles. Therefore, the eyes remain closed and the patient cannot be aroused.[23]

A coma can lead to the patient's recovery or to a vegetative state. It can also lead to the patient's death, usually within a span of two to four weeks.

In essence, patients in a coma are unconscious because they lack both wakefulness and awareness. Patients in a vegetative state are also unconscious because of their lack of awareness, even though they are wakeful.

---

[23] Cf. The Multi-Society Task Force on PVS, "Aspects of Persistent Vegetative State," *NEJM*, 1499-1508

## 8) Can an unconscious human being feel, hear or experience his surroundings?

Since unconsciousness which (characterizes both a coma and a vegetative state) implies global or total unawareness of self and the environment, an unconscious person cannot feel or experience suffering.

Nevertheless, from a medical perspective, many conditions could be confused with total unconsciousness such as, for example, the so-called "Locked-In Syndrome" or the "de-efferented state."[24]

In 1995, a California woman named Kate Adamson suffered a rare double brainstem stroke at the age of 33. Kate was left completely paralyzed for 70 days. She was unable to blink her eyes, let alone speak.

But Kate *could* hear. And she clearly heard the medical staff as they made plans to remove her gastric feeding tube and thereby starve her to death.

Kate had her tube removed for eight horrifying days, but she lived to tell about it, and she recovered

---

[24] According to the Healthlink web site for the Medical College of Wisconsin, "Locked-in syndrome [aka, de-efferented state] is a rare neurological disorder characterized by complete paralysis of voluntary muscles in all parts of the body (except for those that control eye movement). It may result from traumatic brain injury, vascular diseases, demyelinating diseases, or medication overdose."

significantly from her paralysis.

"I could feel everything the doctors did to me, and I could do nothing. I was at the complete mercy of others, and they couldn't hear me," she said.

Her experience is a warning to side with prudence when deciding what to do when a person is declared "unconscious."

## 9) Is an unconscious human being who cannot communicate still a person?

Yes, definitely. As a being created in the image and likeness of God, with intelligence and a will, one's human existence is integrally linked to his or her spiritual existence. Human beings never lose this. To think any other way, that is, to believe that there are circumstances that alter the dignity of men or women as children of God, is to agree with history's most inhumane ideologies, from Nazism to communism.

Furthermore, to believe that an unconscious human is no longer a person would mean that when we sleep, we are no longer human beings until we wake up again. Likewise, according to this line of thought, if someone were to murder a sleeping human being, the murderer wouldn't really have killed anyone. Such lines of reasoning are obviously absurd.

Being unconscious or being incapable of communicating doesn't mean that a human being stops being rational, or that he or she no longer has a will. Rather, it only means the person currently lacks the normal functioning of those traits.

# 10) What is euthanasia?

To answer this question, it's important to state that current usage of term euthanasia has different meanings that are sometimes confusing and contradictory. Thus, the term euthanasia indiscriminately refers to any of the following decisions: to advance the end of a life that is considered "unworthy" (whether due to illness or old age); to use pain control in a terminally ill patient; or to voluntarily refuse therapies that are considered useless or disproportionate.[25]

This ambiguity makes it imperative to clearly specify the definition of euthanasia so that Catholics may understand how it should be judged.

Euthanasia is a word derived from two Greek terms: *eu* meaning beautiful or good and *thanatos* meaning death, that is, beautiful or good death.

The common understanding of euthanasia is "an

---

[25] Ignatio Carrasco de Paula, "Euthanasia," *Lexicon: Ambiguous and Debatable Terms Regarding Family Life and Ethical Questions*, ed. Pontifical Council for the Family, n. 25 (Bologna, 2003). See also Sacred Congregation for the Doctrine of the Faith, "Declaration on Euthanasia," II: *Acta Apostolicae Sedis* 72 (5 May 1980). See
http://www.vatican.va/roman_curia/congregations/cfaith/documents/rc_con_cf aith_doc_19800505_euthanasia_en.html

action or omission which of itself and by intention causes death, with the purpose of eliminating all suffering."[26]

A distinction is sometimes made between active euthanasia, when an intentional act provokes the death of a patient, and passive euthanasia, when a patient is intentionally allowed to die by the omission of care or reasonable and necessary treatments .

Such a distinction is merely descriptive and has no importance from a moral perspective, as both "types" of euthanasia are equally worthy of condemnation.

However, it is important to distinguish between voluntary euthanasia, which is carried out with the patient's consent, and involuntary euthanasia, which is carried out without the patient's consent or request.
Though both are morally objectionable, the latter is more serious.[27]

A term related to euthanasia is disthanasia. Disthanasia can be understood as death that takes place under cruel circumstances, with discomfort, pain and suffering. For example, a death that occurs with inadequate pain

---

[26] John Paul II, encyclical *Evangelium Vitae (EV)*, 65 (25 March 1995). See http://www.vatican.va/edocs/ENG0141/_INDEX.HTM. See also Congregation for the Doctrine of the Faith, "Declaration on Euthanasia," *AAS* 72, II
[27] Cf. *EV*, 66

control or a death associated with pointless and sometimes painful interventions, would be called disthanasia.

Nonetheless, to avoid confusion and misunderstanding, it's preferable to focus on the idea of euthanasia itself.

# 11) Why is euthanasia considered murder?

Euthanasia is considered murder because it always involves the deliberate elimination of a human being; this "rules out any type of similarity to other forms of involuntary homicide."[28] In other words, it always implies the intent to kill another person.[29]

Euthanasia does not eliminate suffering, but instead eliminates the person who suffers. That is why Pope John Paul II stated that it is morally unacceptable and a serious violation of God's law. He reminded us that "this doctrine is based upon the natural law and upon the written word of God, is transmitted by the Church's Tradition and taught by the ordinary and universal Magisterium."[30]

Numerous Church documents of various types condemn euthanasia. The Second Vatican Council's *Pastoral Constitution on the Church in the Modern World: Gaudium et Spes*[31] and Pope John Paul II's encyclical

---

[28] Carrasco, "Euthanasia," *Lexicon.*

[29] Cf., Congregation for the Doctrine of the Faith, "Declaration on Euthanasia," *Iura et Bona* (5 May 1980), II: AAS 72 (1980), 546

[30] Cf., *EV*, 65

[31] Second Vatican Council, *Pastoral Constitution on the Church in the Modern World: Gaudium et Spes*, 27 (7 December 1965). See
http://www.vatican.va/archive/hist_councils/ii_vatican_council/documents/vat-ii_cons_19651207_gaudium-et-spes_en.html

*Dominum et Vivificantem*[32] refer to euthanasia as "an infamy." The *Catechism of the Catholic Church* calls it "homicide."[33] Pope John Paul II's apostolic exhortation *Christifideles Laici* classifies it as "criminal,"[34] and the encyclical *Veritatis Splendor* calls it "a disgrace."[35]

Some years back, the Church's Sacred Congregation for the Doctrine of the Faith condemned euthanasia in a specific document entitled *Declaration on Euthanasia.* In this document, euthanasia was called an "act of killing."[36]

---

[32] John Paul II, Encyclical *Dominum et Vivificantem*, 43 (18 May 1986). See http://www.vatican.va/edocs/ ENG0142/_INDEX.HTM

[33] Cf. *Catechism of the Catholic Church*, 2277 (Vatican City: Libreria Editrice Vaticana, 1993). See

http://www.vatican.va/archive/ENG0015/_INDEX.HTM

[34] Cf. John Paul II, apostolic exhortation *Christifideles Laici*, 38 (30 December 1988). See

http://www.vatican.va/holy_father/john_paul_ii/apost_exhortations/documents /hf_jp-ii_exh_30121988_ christifideles-laici_en.html

[35] John Paul II, encyclical *Veritatis Splendor*, 80 (6 August 1993). See http://www.vatican.va/edocs /ENG0222/ _INDEX.HTM

[36] Congregation for the Doctrine of the Faith, "Declaration on Euthanasia," *Iura et Bona* (5 May 1980), II: AAS 72 (1980), 546

## 12) Wouldn't it be good to legalize euthanasia so that people could die with dignity?

No. Legalizing euthanasia would mean we have the right to directly take the life of someone who is ill, that is, to kill the innocent. This directly contradicts the principle of respect for life. In this case, the life of an innocent person is destroyed, which is gravely wrong even if the person requests it.

The agony of a terminal illness or the suffering of a person who endures a long infirmity do not constitute "undignified" situations, as euthanasia supporters claim. Circumstances of human suffering are truly distressing, but they do not change the fact that the human life continues to have dignity in and of itself and merits our respect without regard to the circumstances surrounding it. An innocent human life must never be eliminated through the direct action of anyone.

Nothing could be more undignified than killing the innocent.

Historically, the legalization and implementation of euthanasia has led to the most barbaric abuses and aberrations imaginable (under the guise of a supposedly good thing, that is, "mercy killing").

It must not be forgotten that the Nazis practiced euthanasia to a massive degree, first, in the case of the terminally ill, then the handicapped, then those with Down's Syndrome, then those who suffered from some type of physical or mental limitation. A supposedly good intention thus led to one of the most atrocious horrors of all human history.

# 13) What does a dignified death mean for a Catholic?

A dignified death is the end of one's human existence that respects the person's spiritual nature. Death occurs without human intervention. A dignified death is one that recognizes that man is a creature who comes from God at the beginning of his existence and returns to Him at the end. It allows him to die, so far as possible, in possession of his faculties, surrounded by those who love him, and comforted and aided by the spiritual and sacramental gifts of his Faith.

If a person is eliminated through euthanasia, no external circumstance changes the fact that he or she is being killed. We often hear of people who are eliminated by removing their nutrition but who are surrounded by their favorite memories or music at the hour of death. In such a circumstance, maudlin sentimentality has come to replace moral truth which instructs us that we may never directly take the life of an innocent human being. Even the pagan physican Hippocrates recognized this when he said in his oath, "I will give no one a deadly medicine even if asked, nor counsel any such thing."

A death is only dignified when it respects the essential dignity of the person as someone created by God.

❧

## 14) What medical means may be applied to sustain the life of a patient whose life is at risk?

The methods used on a patient whose life is at risk may be categorized as either ethically ordinary or ethically extraordinary. Such methods should be distinguished from medically ordinary and extraordinary measures. Medically ordinary methods are those which are scientifically established, statistically successful and reasonably available. Those methods that do not meet these criteria are medically extraordinary. A method which is medically ordinary might be ethically extraordinary. The ethically extraordinary nature of any given method is determined by various criteria: the type of means, the degree of risk, the difficulty of access for those who may request it, its high cost, the increase of suffering it may cause the patient, and a comparison of these factors relative to the expected outcome for the particular patient.[36] If after making this comparison, the various factors considered are disproportionate to the foreseen results, then the method can be morally optional, i.e., not morally obligatory.

Ethically ordinary methods of sustaining life would

---

[36] Cf. Elio Sgreccia, *Manuale di Bioetica [Manual of Bioethics]*, vol. I, 736-7 (Milan: Vita e Pensiero, 2000); see also Congregation for the Doctrine of the Faith, "Declaration on Euthanasia," *AAS* 72, IV

include those that are proportionate to the foreseen results within the parameters just mentioned. We could say they typically include regularly and commonly offered methods of healthcare such as the great majority of pharmaceutical drugs (antibiotics, anti-inflammatories and drugs used to combat hypertension, among others) and various types of surgical intervention.

From a moral perspective, we have an obligation to use ordinary methods to help a dying patient. At the same time, with the patient's consent or upon the patient's request, it is permissible to refuse extraordinary methods of sustaining life, even when such a refusal indirectly advances the patient's death.[37]

As one can appreciate from the given definitions, there is no precise dividing line for categorizing one method as ethically ordinary and another as ethically extraordinary. For example, there may be variations according to the socioeconomic context in which we find ourselves. What is ordinary in an economically solvent society may be extraordinary in an economically troubled one.

---

[37] Cf. Pontifical Council "Cor Unum," *Questions of Ethics Regarding the Fatally Ill and the Dying*, 2.4.3. (27 June 1981). See also Sgreccia, *Manuale*, 736-7

In addition, as science progresses, various methods that were previously considered medically extraordinary have become medically ordinary.

Moreover, it must be recognized that the use of medically extraordinary methods has saved many lives. Currently, therefore, the criterion based on the ethically ordinary or ethically extraordinary nature of the methods still holds[38] and does not include the external "quality of life" standard.

In this respect, our most beloved Pope John Paul II offered important criteria for judging how to confront this moral dilemma. He clearly explained, "First of all, no evaluation of costs can outweigh the value of the fundamental good which we are trying to protect, that of human life. Moreover, to admit that decisions regarding man's life can be based on the external acknowledgment of its quality is the same as acknowledging that increasing and decreasing levels of quality of life, and therefore of human dignity, can be attributed from an external perspective to any subject, thus introducing into social relations a discriminatory and eugenic principle."[39]

❧

---

[38] Congregation for the Doctrine of the Faith, "Declaration on Euthanasia," *AAS* 72, IV

[39] John Paul II, "Address to Congress on 'Life-Sustaining Treatments and Vegetative State,'" 5.

# 15) What are proportionate and disproportionate methods for a person at risk of dying?

The terms ethically ordinary and extraordinary are interchangeable with the terms ethically proportionate and disproportionate as they apply to life-sustaining methods. *The Ethical and Religious Directives for Catholic Health Care Services*, n. 56, defines ethically ordinary or proprotionate means of sustaining life in this way:

> A person has a moral obligation to use ordinary or proportionate means of preserving his or her life. Proportionate means are those that in the judgment of the patient offer a reasonable hope of benefit and do not entail an excessive burden or impose excessive expense on the family or the community.[40]

Ethically extraordinary or disproportionate means are defined in this way by the *Ethical and Religious Directives for Catholic Health Care Services*, n. 57:

> A person may forego extraordinary or

---

[40] United States Conference of Catholic Bishops, *Ethical and Religious Directives for Catholic Health Care Services* (15 June 2001)

disproportionate means of preserving life. Disproportionate means are those that in the patient's judgment do not offer a reasonable hope of benefit or entail an excessive burden, or impose excessive expense on the family or the community.

Therefore, a medically ordinary method may not always be ethically proportionate in all situations to which it may be theoretically applied.

For example, a mechanical respirator used in the case of a young person suffering from transitory paralysis of the respiratory muscles would be an ethically proportionate method of preserving his life.[41] At the same time, that very same respirator would be an ethically disproportionate method for a patient with rampant lung cancer that has totally overridden the lungs and spread throughout the body.

In the second case, using the respirator would not produce any proportionate benefit in the patient's health. It is therefore understandable how the same method can be either ethically proportionate or disproportionate, depending on the concrete situation

---

[41] Such is the case, for example, in patients with Guillain-Barré Syndrome or those who are being treated for tetanus.

with which we are confronted.

Refusing to use an ethically disproportionate method is an expression of acceptance of the human condition in the face of death and is in no way equivalent to suicide or euthanasia.[42] It is important, then, to know how to distinguish when a given method is proportionate and when it is disproportionate.

---

[42] Cf., *EV*, 65

## 16) Must all existing methods be used to keep a patient alive, even when this may imply unnecessary suffering?

The answer is no. In recent times medical science has succeeded in developing interventions that allow death to be artificially delayed with no real benefit to the patient, or even worse, at the cost of further and severe suffering.

These situations have recently become more common, involving so-called therapeutic tyranny or aggressive medical treatment which consist of "the use of methods which are particularly exhausting and painful for the patient, condemning him in fact to an artificially prolonged agony."[43]

Such methods or medical procedures "no longer correspond to the real situation of the patient, either because they are by now disproportionate to any expected results or because they impose an excessive burden on the patient and his family."[44]

Aggressive medical treatment under these circumstances is neither justifiable nor acceptable from

---

[43] John Paul II, "To the Participants at the International Congress on Assistance to the Dying," *L'Osservatore Romano*, n. 4 (18 March 1992). See also Pontifical Council for Pastoral Assistance, *Charter*, p. 119; *EV*, 65
[44] *EV*, 65

any perspective. When death is clearly imminent and inevitable, one may in good conscience "refuse forms of treatment that would only secure a precarious and burdensome prolongation of life, so long as the normal care due to the sick person in similar cases is not interrupted."[45]

The decision to forego aggressive medical treatment is not euthanasia and must be distinguished from it; neither is it suicide.[46] Rather, it simply involves acceptance of death.

---

[45] Congregation for the Doctrine of the Faith, "Declaration on Euthanasia," *AAS* 72, IV. See also *EV*, 65

[46] Cf., *EV*, 65

# 17) What is palliative medicine?

Palliative medicine or palliative therapy, which is used in terminal illnesses when the possibility of a cure no longer exists, seeks to alleviate the patient's symptoms and accompany him or her in death. Among the various forms of palliative care, analgesics and sedatives to control pain play an important role.[47]

For example, treatment for the symptoms of widespread cancer is considered palliative. In this regard, the Catholic Church declared several decades ago[48] that the use of narcotics to subdue pain is permissible when other medications are not available. Even though narcotics may limit consciousness and may indirectly shorten the lifespan as a consequence of their use, they are permitted as long as they do not prevent the patient from fulfilling his or her religious or moral duties.

Palliative therapy is included within the methods of palliative care "which seek to make suffering more bearable in the final stages of illness and to ensure that the patient is supported and accompanied in his or her ordeal."[49]

---

[47] Cf., Clayman, *AMA Encyclopedia of Medicine.* See also Pontifical Council for Pastoral Assistance, *Charter*, p. 117

[48] Pius XII, "Address on 'Reanimation.'"

[49] *EV*, 65

Palliative medicine neither prolongs life nor causes death. It does not seek to eliminate the *patient* but rather the suffering or pain that afflicts him. It also attempts to provide the patient a sense of comfort and well-being. Such palliative methods of treatment are initiated in the presence of a reverent, generous and attentive health care worker who serves the terminally ill in a way that "gives confidence and hope to patients and makes them reconciled to death."[50]

---

[50] Pontifical Council for Pastoral Assistance, *Charter,* p. 117. See also "Cor Unum," *Questions of Ethics*, 4.3

# 18) What type of care should a person in a coma or a vegetative state receive?

Because of their health condition, individuals in a vegetative state or coma rely completely on those who care for and assist them. However, as we have previously stated, neither of these health conditions causes a patient to lose his status or significance as a person, and the patient must therefore receive the corresponding care.

Any applicable palliative treatments should be given to the patient in hopes of either recovery, providing ethically proportionate care for an indefinite period, or the arrival of natural death.

Each of these patients "still has the right to basic health care (nutrition, hydration, cleanliness, warmth, etc.), and to the prevention of complications related to his confinement to bed,"[51] such as bedsores. They should also have recourse to the proper hygiene that is physiologically necessary to human beings.

Moreover, because of their clinical condition, these patients have "the right to appropriate rehabilitative care and to be monitored for clinical signs of eventual recovery."[52]

[51] John Paul II, "Address to Congress on 'Life-Sustaining Treatments and Vegetative State,'" 4

[52] Ibid.

## 19) What form of care should be given to a person with a degenerative disease that is non-fatal in the short term?

Patients with degenerative illnesses that are non-fatal in the short term often pose the question of how they will live out the final stages of their life, and how they will arrive at death. Beyond the fear of death itself, they are afraid of how they are going to die. With palliative care, especially adequate pain control, symptom management, and human companionship, these patients have at their disposal all the necessary means to guarantee them quality end-of-life care, with a dignified and peaceful approach to the end of their lives.

This will allow them to fulfill their moral and family obligations, and especially to prepare themselves in a full state of consciousness – with a good and clear moral conscience – for their definitive encounter with God.

The wave of emotions which accompanies the diagnosis of a degenerative illness may very well lead the patient, in human frailty, to wish death upon himself. Let us recall that such a thought is "not to be understood as implying a true desire for euthanasia; in fact, it is almost always a case of an anguished plea for help and love."[53]

Truthfully speaking, those who face an unavoidable future of suffering and death may tend to ask for their life to end,[54] when in fact their actual desire is for companionship and consolation on their difficult journey.

That is why, aside from medical care, these patients should be offered love, "the human and supernatural warmth with which the sick person can and ought to be surrounded by those close to him or her, parents and children, doctors and nurses."[55] These individuals should assure the ill that they will never be abandoned or considered a burden by their loved ones, and that inappropriately prolonging their suffering will be avoided.

---

[53] Congregation for the Doctrine of the Faith, "Declaration on Euthanasia," *AAS* 72, II

[54] Pontifical Council for Pastoral Assistance, *Charter*, p. 149

[55] Congregation for the Doctrine of the Faith, "Declaration on Euthanasia," *AAS* 72, II

## 20) Can the removal of nourishment and hydratation from a terminally ill patient or a person in so-called "persistent vegetative state" be considered morally justifiable?

Nourishment and hydration are part of basic health care or the normal care that must be provided to the terminally ill or to those in a persistent vegetative state. To give food and drink to a person, even artificially, when it is deemed to be ethically proportionate for the person can never be considered "aggressive medical treatment." On the contrary, doing so "always represents a natural means of preserving life, not a medical act, [and] its use, furthermore, should be considered, in principle, ordinary and proportionate"[57] until and to the extent that it is evident the patient has been nourished and that his suffering has thus been alleviated.

Therefore, to interrupt feeding or hydration is not morally justifiable under such circumstances. Indeed, the undue suspension of nourishment or hydration would inevitably cause the patient's death by starvation or dehydration, such that it "could amount to euthanasia in a proper sense."[58]

---

[57] John Paul II, "Address to Congress on 'Life-Sustaining Treatments and Vegetative State,'" 4.

[58] Pontifical Council for Pastoral Assistance, *Charter*, p. 120. See also John Paul II, "Address to Congress on 'Life-Sustaining Treatments and Vegetative State,'" 4.

The fact that the chances of recovery from a persistent vegetative state are slim does not ethically justify the removal of nutrition and hydration from the patient. As studies demonstrate, withdrawing nutrition and hydration may be a source of considerable suffering for these patients.

# 21) What practices do hospitals use that we should avoid because they are immoral?

The end of life is a time when the human person is particularly vulnerable. With advances in technology, death has become "medicalized" and is viewed as a medical defeat, with perhaps growing feelings of guilt over the failure to avoid it.[59]

Such can be the case in hospitals with the so called aggressive medical treatment in the face of inevitable and imminent death. These interventions (which are not truly treatments) submit the patient to a degree of suffering beyond what is necessary, such as repeated attempts at cardiopulmonary resuscitation beyond a reasonable timeframe or the use of artificial respirators when there is no longer any chance for spontaneous respiration or heart activity in the patient.

In this matter it is important that we know how to distinguish if the medical methods utilized are proportionate to the chances for improvement in the patient. Therefore, the attending physician should be seriously questioned regarding the patient's actual medical condition and the treatment methods being utilized in order to determine when to refuse methods

---

[59] Tierney, *Current Medical Diagnosis*, p. 60

that are not proportionate to the patient's situation.

On the other hand, a judgment regarding the patient's quality-of-life, as well as the cost of medical interventions, may determine a hospital's actions, which may in turn lead to the unjustifiable delay or abandonment of a certain treatment, thus causing the elimination of a life.

Using these criteria, let us consider the case of two patients. One patient who is seropositive (i.e., who has HIV) or who suffers from a degenerative illness is involved in a car accident. He is admitted into the hospital with a massive hemorrhage and desperately needs a blood transfusion. A second patient is in a vegetative state and develops pneumonia that causes breathing difficulty. Both patients might become victims of deliberate medical negligence. Various health centers have even developed terminology for this premeditated negligence, which is known as "slow code." When slow code deliberately seeks to delay urgent medical attention in the hopes of causing death, it is immoral.

Such hospital practices do occur and a common factor can be identified in them: The attitude of a doctor who hastens to make a decision on behalf of the patient or on behalf of the family when a patient is incompetent, which is not truly in the best interest of the patient.

Here once again, we must be careful to ensure that the patient is offered all methods of treatment that are proportionate to his or her particular medical condition.

In light of this, the patient (as long as he or she is conscious) and his family members (when the patient becomes incompetent because of a medical condition) must be alert and keep a permanent, open dialogue with the doctor and other health personnel. As an additional alternative that allows patients to safeguard themselves from these morally reprehensible hospital practices, the Advance Medical Directive has been established.

## 22) What is an Advance Medical Directive?

One type of Advance Medical Directive, also known as a living will, is a written document with legal ramifications "by which each individual must expressly indicate how he or she wishes to be treated in the event that he or she should encounter a critical, or in any way terminal, situation."[60]

More specifically, this document explains which medical procedures the patient would like to receive or avoid in case he or she should become incompetent such as cardiopulmonary resuscitation in the event of cardiorespiratory failure (that is, when the heart and lungs stop functioning because of some illness or accident).

The living will, then, seeks to define the moral limits by which any medical intervention must be bound.

The living will should thus constitute a free expression of the patient's will according to the patient's legitimate autonomy exercised for his benefit in accord with the moral law, which is praiseworthy and one of the four basic principles of bioethics.

---

[60] Carrasco, "Euthanasia," *Lexicon*.

However, it is very important to specify that in focusing on who will make the decisions in the final moments of the person's life (that is, if it will be the patient - or whoever he or she has designated in the living will - or if it will be the doctors), there is a risk of losing sight of what must be permitted or avoided regarding the patient's welfare. (An advance medical directive that accounts for this need is called a health care proxy or a durable power of attorney for health care.)

Unfortunately, this fact makes the living will an ambiguous tool because with it, one may choose and request different available therapies while running the very real risk of falling into futile interventions. Likewise, the living will may secure the patient's wish to refuse medical intervention of any type, even to the point of requesting collaboration from the doctor in executing the "right to die," that is, euthanasia.[61] There is no "right" to refuse treatment which would be beneficial and thus morally obligatory.

---

[61] Sgreccia, *Manuale*, 218

# 23) May a Catholic execute a living will?

A living will in and of itself is not contrary to proper morals, and a Catholic may therefore make use of this document. However, given its ambiguity relative to its possible ends, some of which are not morally permissible, if a Catholic utilizes this document, he or she should do so reasonably, in accordance with the faith he or she professes and with Church teachings regarding death and the dignity of the dying person.

A Catholic's living will must be a tool which, in the moment of need, contributes to the patient's "happy death," experienced with complete tranquility and with Christian and human dignity.

# 24) What should a Catholic's living will be like?

In light of what we have presented to this point, a Catholic's living will should above all utilize clear language that is free from any ambiguity in all of its affirmations. In this way interpretative errors will be avoided by the doctors or by those responsible for the patient's care.

Above all, a proper living will for a Catholic will insist that he or she be regarded as a person and that his or her dignity as a human being will be recognized up until the natural end of life. The document must explicitly exclude any form of euthanasia, as well as reject an abusive and irrational extension of the death process.

It must also insist that the patient receive medical treatments that are proportionate to his or her clinical situation, with no therapeutic cruelty, neglect or the withdrawal of normal methods of care such as nutrition, hydration, shelter or warmth.

The document should further request that all necessary medical and nursing care be utilized to treat the patient, even when the goal is only to provide comfort. In this context, the patient may request to be relieved of physical and other types of suffering through the use of sedatives and analgesics, even though this may limit consciousness or indirectly shorten the lifespan. Moreover, the living will should insist on assistance in fulfilling the patient's moral and religious duties, such that it should state the patient's right to participate in religious practices (such as the sacraments) in a timely fashion, and to be in the company of family members.

# 25) How much suffering must a terminally ill Christian tolerate?

Suffering accompanies our very existence. We all suffer, and for various reasons: the death of a loved one, defeat or failure, loneliness, misunderstanding, abuse or outrage by others, and, obviously, physical discomfort.

But suffering cannot be compared to the gift of life, because life involves richness, fulfillment and promise. Suffering, on the other hand, is the echo of deprivation, the repercussion of evil in our life experience. Suffering exists because evil exists because it, in turn, entered the world with original sin.

Pope John Paul II reminded us, "God does not want sickness; He did not create evil or death."[62] Neither does God desire suffering. But Jesus took suffering upon Himself in order to change it into Redemption. By His wounds, we are healed (cf. Is 53:8-12; I Pt 2:18-21). This thought sheds light on the current situation and helps us to answer our own question. Through Christ, suffering now has meaning. No longer is it an absurdity, but instead it can be a means to redemption. St. Paul says, "What is lacking in the sufferings of

---

[62] John Paul II, Angelus address, 1 (13 February 2000). See www.vatican.va/holy_father/john_paul_ii/angelus/2000/documents/hf_jp-ii_ang_20000213_en.html

Christ I fill up in my flesh for His body, which is the Church" (Col 1:24). When the sufferings of the terminally ill are united to Christ's sufferings in order to help others save themselves, they are not useless. All suffering whether great or small that is patiently endured over the course of one's life has tremendous value in God's eyes, as in some way it enters into the suffering endured by His Son, Jesus Christ.

The hedonistic culture in which we live is scandalized by suffering and rejects it. But as we have already seen, doing so is to reject existence itself, and that is impossible. Attempting to live without suffering is to live deceived, to live a lie.

The truly conscientious Christian understands that suffering, in its various degrees, is a part of life and that not only can it be patiently endured thanks to the gift of faith and the power of the sacraments, but it can also have redemptive value when united to the cross of Christ.

## 26) Isn't it more merciful and Christian to facilitate the death of a suffering person?

No. It could never be merciful or Christian to kill an innocent person or to "facilitate" death (that is, too directly accelerate death) for someone who deserves care and respect from us in his suffering.

What is truly merciful and Christian is to accompany the person in his suffering, to pray for him and to spiritually unite ourselves to his pain, keeping in mind that his approaching death signifies his arrival at an existence where suffering will no longer exist.

## 27) What type of pastoral care should a terminally ill patient receive?

When a terminally ill patient is conscious, he should be helped to prepare himself for his encounter with God. Proper pastoral care should strive to help him discover a way of using his sufferings to unite himself to Christ. And once accepting and fully taking on his situation, the patient should be helped to understand that his existence is valuable because it is offered for the good of others.

Above all, the man or woman who is suffering has the right to understand the circumstances, reasons and conditions of that suffering. Only in discovering the truth of one's own life will a person be able to accept and assimilate that truth.

Accepting suffering is often more difficult than enduring it. Many profound questions naturally come up about the person himself and about God. "Why me?" and "Why did this happen to me?" are some of the questions triggered by suffering.

Pastoral companionship must, above all, help the person to comprehend that suffering is not necessarily a "punishment," but a reality which is at the same time a great mystery; that it can only be interpreted as a "curse" in the eyes of the world, but not in the eyes of our faith that believes in a Redeemer who died on the cross for us.

Through constant, loving support and an appeal that he see reality with eyes of faith, the patient must be helped to fight off bitterness and feelings of rejection. These emotions lead nowhere; they are fruitless and wind up poisoning the sick person and those around him.

The terminally ill should be the object of all the Church's affection and diligence through the sacraments and the prayers of other Catholics.

As we have said, the Church does not prohibit the use of medication to alleviate suffering, even if doing so should indirectly shorten the remaining days of the terminally ill, as long as "death is not willed as either an end or a means, but only foreseen and tolerated as inevitable" (*Catechism of the Catholic Church*, 2279).

A terminally ill person who is unconscious also has the right to full pastoral and charitable care from the Church and those who surround him. He should not be treated as an annoying "thing" that should be disposed of as quickly as possible.

Above all other possible forms of care, the dying person should receive the sacrament of Anointing of the Sick with Confession and the reception of the Holy Eucharist and should be accompanied by prayers and nurturing until the moment he departs.

## 28) What type of pastoral care should a patient with a degenerative disease receive?

A person suffering from a degenerative disease should be attended to in a special way, since his physical strength and psychological capacity gradually decrease until they practically disappear or can no longer be externally manifested.

Such a person should be accompanied by charity and attended to with love, since God wants His love to shine and manifest itself in our charitable acts. The person should be invited to pray as much as possible, associating his sufferings with those of Christ (cf., Col 1:24), and he should receive the sanctifying grace that prepares him for his meeting with God.

# 29) What attitude should Catholics have when confronted with death?

In the face of death, Catholics should be conscious of two things. First of all, death is a consequence of sin (as it says in Scripture and Tradition, and as the Magisterium teaches). God created man to be immortal (cf., Wis 2:23f), but because of original sin, death and pain became part of our existence (cf., Rom 5:12f), thus marking the beginning of our pilgrimage of pain and suffering.

Therefore, fear or rejection of death and longing to live forever are both real and, in a certain sense, natural aspects of our various life experiences.

Second of all, the Lord Jesus has given death new meaning. It is no longer a meaningless end to a painful existence, nor is it the definitive step that carries us into nothingness.

Through Jesus, who freely chose to die for us, death has become a means of redemption and reconciliation. Therefore, it marks the passage into an existence that can be truly complete and happy, because through love, we have prepared ourselves for our definitive encounter with God.

We can say, "Because of Christ, Christian death has a positive meaning" (*Catechism of the Catholic Church*, 1010).

Furthermore, although "the certainty of death saddens us" (Canon of the Mass), we know that life does not end with death, but rather, it can be the beginning of a complete and perfect existence and of true happiness. For death will lead us to God where we can live happily together with Him and with our brothers and sisters for all eternity. This should cause us to reflect upon our lives, to improve our lives, and to straighten our steps according to the ways of truth and love, that is, according to God's ways. In this way our end will be a good one. St. Augustine said, *"Sicut vita, finis ita"* (As your life is, thus will your end be). Our attitude toward death should make us appreciate our life and to live it fully according to the loving plan that God has prepared for each one of us.

# 30) What is a culture of life?

We know that culture is the way in which men and women in a community mold or shape a particular way of relating to nature, to each other and to God, thus establishing a typical style of human coexistence.

Culture includes all the ways in which mankind manifests itself: values, vices, and in social, political, artistic and religious structures. As Pope John Paul II said during his pastoral visit to Los Angeles, culture is all those things that reflect the soul of a nation.

Man's relationship with God is thus an essential element of culture. Pope John Paul II stated that culture is the fruit of mankind. At the same time, it humanizes mankind. Thus, culture is "man's dwelling place."

Unfortunately, culture may also express the destructive elements in human existence, such as man's experiences of sin and evil. Therefore, cultural expressions of sin such as war, violence in all its forms, hedonism, consumerism, atheism, etc., will inevitably exist.

Pope John Paul II referred to this type of "anti-culture" as the "culture of death" because it manifests itself in ways that lead to the oppression and annihilation of human beings. Therefore, in opposition to the "culture of death," the Holy Father offered a "culture of life," which is a cultural expression that defends the dignity of human life in all its forms and thus rescues culture's most essential element (i.e., man's relationship with God). The "culture of life" places itself at the disposal of men and women in order to properly orient them toward their true potential.

One of the primary values of the "culture of life" is respect for life from its beginning at conception until its natural end. It also emphasizes the important conviction that it is the Lord Jesus who reveals the type of perfection God is inviting us to, so that we may have life and have it in abundance.

When a culture is capable of protecting and encouraging this vision of mankind through its political, social, economic and legal structures, it can be called a "culture of life".

Building such a culture not only requires the collaboration of society's leaders, but it is also a duty and a right of all Christians. A father or mother contributes to the culture of life by educating their children about the value of life as a gift from God; a priest contributes by defending and preaching about the value of life; a young person can help to build the culture of life by announcing the Gospel of Life to his friends and companions without letting himself be overcome by fear.

As Catholics, in every circumstance, we must do all we can to build a culture of life.

We would like to know how this book
helped you in your journey of faith.
Please address all mail to:

Basilica Press
111 Ferguson Court
Suite 102
Irving, TX 75062

To get a free resource catalogue of
other Basilica Press books and
tapes, please contact:

www.BasilicaPress.com

Or call us toll-free at

**1-800-933-9398**